S0-AKA-489

Sergio Cartocci

Tivoli

The Tiburtine area:
its history
and works of art

Villa d'Este
Villa Gregoriana
Villa Adriana

ART PUBLISHERS
ROME

Index

© Copyright by **KOSMO**
Text and graphic art by Sergio Cartocci
Translation by Harold Dunster

Tibur superbum

This publication, by no means the first to have been produced about Tivoli, is not intended to improve the mind. But it is intended to please the eye, since the publishers, OTO Edizioni d'Arte, have adopted an essentially visual approach, with the inclusion of numerous illustrations and descriptive captions. Perhaps one of the greatest merits of this form of presentation is that it is acceptable also to those whose knowledge of history and the arts has become a little rusty. And so it is a work for people of all ages and all levels of erudition.

It will be particularly appreciated by the tourist who, as is often the case nowadays, has only a limited amount of time for his excursions. And when he returns home he will find no difficulty in turning to a place or a work that aroused his special interest during his visit: it will be at once a souvenir and, by virtue of its attractive presentation, a valuable addition to his bookshelf.

Besides providing a concise history of Tivoli, the publication evokes the original magnificence of Hadrian's Villa, revives the splendours of Villa d'Este of the Renaissance period and describes the nineteenth-century restoration of Villa Gregoriana. Tivoli is justly proud of these prodigious monuments: the first, the Emperor Hadrian's highest exaltation of the Roman

Empire; the second, the realization of the dream of a Prince of the Church of Rome; the third, the exquisite expression of Papal culture. In their respective ways these authorities succeeded in creating works of outstanding artistic, social and cultural interest whose importance has been neither dimmed nor diminished with the passage of time.
As he turns the pages of this book the reader will find himself becoming absorbed in a past that is everlastingly topical.

Prof. CARLO BERARDI
Director of Villa d'Este

History of Tivoli

One day some twenty thousand years ago a man sat carving the image of a wolf on a stone of a grotto close to Ponte Lucano: this was the beginning of the known history of the Tiburtine territory, which already in those times, by virtue of its position, abundance of water and game, healthiness of clime, must have been an ideal area in which to live.

Situated in a half-moon of the lower foothills of the Apennines facing the Tyrrhenian Sea, like an easily defended citadel towering over the Aniene valley, an outpost looking on to the Abruzzi mountains, a magnificent balcony overhanging the Roman plain, the area in which Tibur (the Latin name for Tivoli) arose embraced all the strategic and residential attributes which were to link its history so intimately with that of the splendid Rome stretched at its feet.

Tivoli is situated 31 km to the east of the capital, on Via Tiburtina-Valeria, astride the River Aniene, which on its way from the Simbruini hills towards the Tiber narrows between Colle Ripoli and Monte Catillo, forming the awesome gorges through which its water cascades over the picturesque falls. The origins of Tivoli, shrouded in the mists of time, began to reveal themselves with the discovery of the palaeolithic stone (A. M. Radmilli, 1953), now kept in Rome's Pigorini Ethnological Museum. Other discoveries of the neolithic period and the bronze age (approximately 5,000 years ago) indicate the presence of prehistoric man throughout the area. Perhaps they were bands of hunters who had come down from the Sabine hills and Abruzzi mountains, pioneering the route of what later became Via Valeria, crossing the Aniene at the Acquonia ford.

▲
The armorial bearings and standards of the four municipal districts of Tivoli, each of which is divided into wards.

Rocca Pia ▶
Begun in 1461 by Pius II Piccolomini on an old walled fortress, it was completed by Alessandro VI Borgia, grandfather of Ippolito d'Este. Here, on 3 September 1539, Paul III received S. Ignatius of Loyola to approve the founding rules of the Jesuits.

Temples of Vesta and the Sibyl ▶
The well-preserved 18 Corinthian column circular temple dedicated to the worship of Vesta dates back to the 1st cent. B. C. and is considered a town symbol. Alongside is the 2nd cent. B. C. rectangular Ionic temple formerly dedicated to worship of the famous Albunea Sibyl.

But around 1000 B. C., at the beginning of the iron age, the first inhabited localities arose, created probably by Latium and Sabine people, joined later by Etruscans, Siculi and Greeks. In Latin writings various theories are advanced as to the origin of Tibur: Cato the Censor in the 2nd century B. C., and later Solino in the 3rd century, attribute the foundation of the town to Tiburto, son of Catillo of Arcadia, a Greek refugee; Antioco Siracusano, instead, claimed in the 5th century B. C. that it was founded by the Siculi in 1215 B. C., while Diodoro Siculo, in the 1st century B. C., attributed it to Latium and Siculi people, bound by a common tongue.

Whatever its origin, however, Tibur soon joined the alliance known as the « Lega Latina » which, led by Tusculum, held sway over nine towns, in a ruthless long-standing struggle against the spread of Roman power. In 499 B. C. the « Lega » lost the battle of Lago Regillo and was forced to make peace with Rome: but the Latium towns rose in rebellion and Tibur allied itself with the Gauls who invaded the Tiber valley, and it was only in 339 B. C. that L. Furio Camillo succeeded in obtaining the definitive submission of Latium. From then on, while retaining a certain measure of autonomy, Tibur's destiny was bound to that of the great Republic, already embarked upon dominion of the old world. In 90 B. C. the *Lex Julia* conferred Roman citizenship on the towns of Latium. Tibur became a municipality and entered into a golden period: its salubrious hills, with abundant water, enticed the Roman patricians to build splendid villas and monuments in the town: the most striking testimony still remaining is the magnificent villa built by the Emperor Hadrian.

With the triumph of Christianity, the pagan religions of Hercules, of Vesta, of Sibylla Tiburtina were gradually abandoned: at Tivoli there are still the remains of large temples, once very much frequented. But the decline of the Roman Empire saw the beginning, also for Tibur, of dark centuries of barbaric invasions. In the massive struggles between the Goths and Byzantines the town was repeatedly sacked and damaged; but from the horrors of war there finally arose the splendid ascetic-humanistic ideal of monasticism. In this Medieval renascence, Tibur played a leading role: at the nearby Subiaco the Benedictine order was founded, and already by the end of the 6th century a number of monasteries had been established at Tivoli. After the Longobard invasion and the agreements with the Byzantines of Ravenna, Tibur became part of the *Ducato Ro-*

The S. Sylvester frescoes

A series of splendid frescoes (second half of 12th century) adorn the triumphal arch and apse of this Romanesque church, much of the structure of which is now unfortunately missing.

The decorative cycle depicts stories of Christ and the legend of S. Sylvester and the Emperor Constantine.

The prehistoric wolf

This carving on a stone found in the Polesini Grotto at Ponte Lucano is some 20,000 years old. Discovered by A.M. Radmilli in 1953, it is the earliest evidence of human life in the Tiburtine area, dating back to the paleolithic period.

mano: and the steady growth of Papal power saw the progressive increase in episcopal influence over the life and destinies of the town. But the Roman Senate would not renounce its authority over the nearby towns, and there is evidence, already in the year 900, of the presence of a Count, the emissary of the *Ducato,* with the purpose of taking over the town. The reaction of the populace led to a reawakening of social conscience, to a diminution of episcopal authority, to a new form of autonomy: a breeze of freedom, of ancient origins, encouraged Tivoli to shrug its shoulders at the rule of Rome. In the struggle between the Papacy and the Empire, the town could do no other but to take sides with the Ghibellines: loyalty to the Emperors meant recognition, protection, autonomy. And so Tivoli prospered, fortified itself, organized itself: of that epoch remain many fine square-towered houses, the typical dwelling-stronghold of the period.

The Municipality adopted as its coat-of-arms an Imperial eagle, to which were added subsequently a bridge and two towers, in recognition of the protection afforded by Barbarossa at Ponte

▲
Anio Novus
Sketch of Tiburtine countryside, by E. Roesler Franz (1845-1907), ardent painter of Tivoli settings.

S. Andrea ▶
Romanesque belltower of the church built on the Temple of Diana, still standing in the year 945.

Christ the Teacher ▶▶
Centrepiece of a precious 12th cent. triptych in the 6th cent. S. Lorenzo Cathedral.

Santa Maria Maggiore
Adjoining Villa d'Este, the 5th cent. church, with 13th cent. Cosmatesque floors, contains the tombs of the Cardinals of the House of Este. ▶

Lucano in 1155. Following the example of the former Roman « regions », the town was divided into the four districts which still exist today: Trevio, San Paolo, Santa Croce and Castrovetere. The struggle with Rome had seen centuries of alternating fortunes: factions, internal power struggles, victories, defeats, not to mention natural calamities such as earthquakes and pestilence.

Then Imperial authority declined: Tivoli, weary, depopulated and disillusioned, found in Papal benevolence the last protection against the incursions of the noble Roman Orsini and Colonna factions. In 1461 Pope Pius II had the turreted Rocca Pia built: it was a symbol of eternal protection, but also a warning to the Tiburtines, and marked the material end of the glorious Comune.

Tivoli gradually became a Papal town: it was here that Ignatius of Loyola founded the Society of Jesus, and in 1550 Pope Julius III appointed the Cardinal of Ferrara, Ippolito d'Este, as Governor of Tivoli. The Cardinals of the House of Este ruled over the city for 75 years, stimulating its artistic renascence, crowned by the jewel, Villa d'Este, which they themselves created. The town was further embellished in the 17th and 18th centuries and thereon was to enjoy relative tranquility and a flourishing cultural life.

After the interval of the Napoleonic Empire (1804-1814), of which Tivoli was an administrative district capital, under the 1816 *motu proprio* of Pius VII, the town became the capital of one of the two districts of the « Comarca » of Rome. During the Italian Risorgimento (leading to the establishment of a single nation State), the old yearnings for freedom from Papal rule re-emerged and the people declared their allegiance to the Roman Republic of 1849. Luigi Coccanari, a Tiburtine patriot, led the revolt, but was exiled when on June 30, 1849, with Garibaldi's retreat to Romagna, the dream of liberty faded. But Coccanari returned to Tivoli in 1860 to head the clandestine National Committee, culminating on September 18, 1870 with the hoisting of the Italian tricolour in Tivoli, two days before Rome capitulated, marking the end of Pontifical temporal sovereignty.

Today the Municipality of Tivoli, which has retained its traditional coat-of-arms of magenta and blue, is an attractive bustling township of 45,000 inhabitants, renowned throughout the world for its testimonies of Imperial and Papal splendour.

▶

Villa d'Este
The avenue of the Hundred Fountains is one of the park's most stupendous. Designed by Pirro Ligorio, the verdant silence of four centuries is broken only by the murmur of water.

The magnificent Villa d'Este

On September 9, 1550 Cardinal Ippolito II d'Este ceremoniously entered Tivoli to take up his appointment as civil Governor of the town. He was the son of Alfonso I d'Este, Duke of Ferrara, and of the notorious Lucrezia Borgia, and was therefore a nephew of Alexander VI Borgia, who left his not always illustrious mark on the history of the Papacy.

Through the intrigues and malpractices of his mother's family, Ippolito was appointed Archbishop of Milan at the tender age of nine, Ambassador to the Paris of Francois I when he was twenty-six, and three years later he was made a cardinal by Pope Paul III. Extremely capable and intelligent, highly ambitious, Ippolito had commenced his ascent to the Papal Throne. But the Medici and Farnese families succeeded in having Julius III elected, and so Ippolito was appointed, to console him in his defeat, Governor of Tivoli.

He never gave up his aspiration to wear the Papal tiara — indeed, he was defeated on a further four occasions — until in 1567, with the election of Pope Pius IV, he was punished for his continuous intrigues by being removed from the Pontifical Curia and he was forced to retire, weary and ill, to Tivoli, where he spent his last years.

The more unworthy side of this man is however, in the light of history, mitigated by his great gifts of culture, of humanism and of patronage inherited from the refined and luxurious environment of his father's palace, and developed during his long acquaintance with the sophistication and brilliance of the European courts of the Renaissance period.

On his arrival in Tivoli, Ippolito II had to stay in the ancient Benedictine monastery, adjoining the Church of S. M. Mag-

▶

The Girandola Fountain
Another Ligorio creation, the fountain takes its name from the catherine-wheel effect devised by Tommaso da Siena. Informed that Gregory XIII wished to visit the Villa, Cardinal Luigi d'Este commissioned Orazio Olivieri to build a monument with four winged dragons (insignia of the Pope's family, the Boncompagni). Completed in record time, the monument was placed in the centre of the basin: from then on the fountain was known as the Fountain of the Dragons.

giore, which had been adapted to become the seat of the Governor: he found the modesty and inadequacy of these quarters quite intolerable. He wished to possess a residence worthy of his rank, and immediately envisaged a grandiose project that was to see, in a short space of time, the conversion of the decrepit convent, and the adjoining area to the north, into one of the most superb princely palaces of the epoch. He entrusted the planning to a renowned Mannerist architect, the Neapolitan Pirro Ligorio: a man of his times, Ligorio designed the vast garden of the villa as an architectural composition, complementary to the palace and the environment, obtaining a perfect harmony both of structure and of perspective. Ligorio immediately planned the conversion and enlargement of the building, and assigned the work to the architect G. A. Galvani of Ferrara: he was then able to devote himself to planning the lay-out of the park. When the building work was completed, the Cardinal commissioned the decoration of the villa to the most distinguished artists of the times, such as Zuccari, Muziano, Agresti.

When Ippolito II died in 1572, the project was almost completed. During the preceding years the villa had been a centre for artists, poets, philosophers, musicians and scientists of such renown that even Pius IV and Gregory XIII could not refuse the hospitality of the grand patron, to renew their spirit in the enchanting shaded paths.

On Ippolito's death the villa passed first to Cardinal Luigi d'Este (1538-1586) and then to Cardinal Alessandro d'Este (1568-1624), who completed his dream. Then, after long disputes with the Papacy, the villa came into the loving possession of the Dukes of Ferrara until it became the property of the Hapsburgs with the marriage of Maria Beatrice, the last descendant of the House of Este, after which it was neglected and abandoned for many long years.

When finally Cardinal Hohenlohe (1823-1896) took possession of the villa, he had it partially restored and some of the former splendour and artistic life returned, especially when the celebrated pianist Franz Liszt was a guest.

In 1919, under the Treaty of St. Germain, the Italian State took possession of Villa d'Este, restored it completely under the direction of Prof. Attilio Rossi, and opened it to the public. From then on the Museums Directorate has maintained the incomparable villa and park in perfect order, and in our times some 1,200,000 visitors every year are entranced by this sublime blend of Italian sixteenth century splendour.

Villa d'Este
An old etching of the planimetry of the villa, and the present siting of the fountains. Formerly, entry was by the centre of the lower gardens, on the road from Rome: nowadays one enters by the palace. Thus, to gain an impression of the real splendour, it is advisable to proceed immediately to the lower gardens, and then return along the avenues and paths back to the villa.

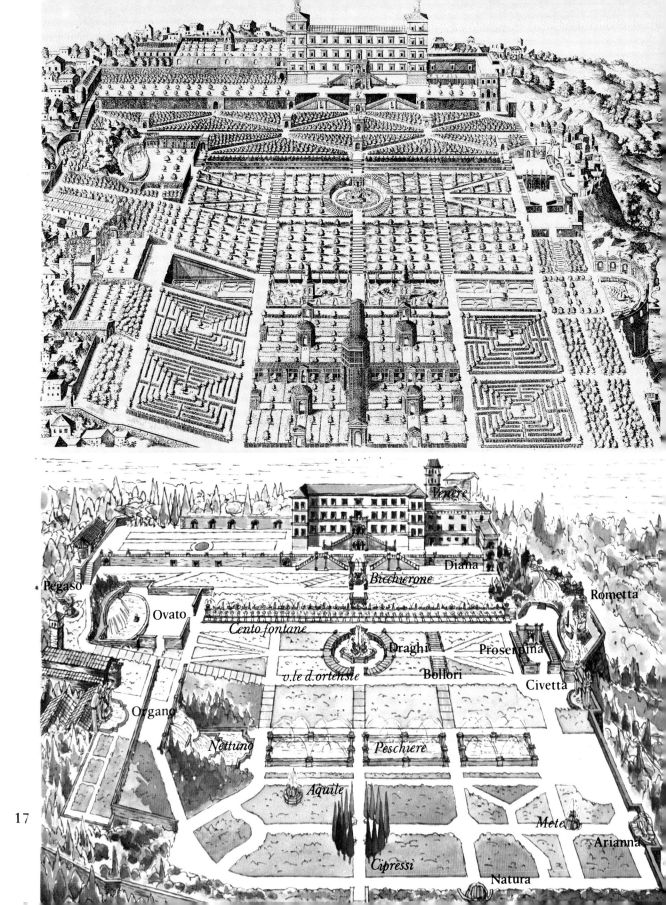

Venere

Diana

Pegaso

Bicchierone

Rometta

Ovato

Cento fontane

Draghi

Proserpina

v.le d.ortensie

Bollori

Civetta

Organo

Nettuno

Peschiere

Aquile

Mete

Arianna

Cipressi

Natura

17

Entrance to Villa from S. M. Maggiore.

Facade overlooking the park and Pallacorda courtyard.

The gardens

When Pirro Ligorio undertook the challenging task of designing Villa d'Este, the fundamental canons of the art of the Italianate garden, understood as a complementary feature of the house, had already been largely established in the 15th century and incorporated in many large 16th century villas. But his talent and instinct enabled him to surpass all other existing examples, with the application of geometry, perspective and architectural principles in the creation of this garden, this masterpiece of hydraulic engineering which still today qualifies Villa d'Este as unique throughout the world. Ligorio ardently resolved a mass of technical problems. He began, in building the garden terrace, by literally sweeping away an entire quarter of the town, Valle Gaudente: then he used the old town walls as buttresses. His radical solution of water-supply involved the excavation, beneath the town, of a tunnel 600 metres long, 1.3 metres wide and 2.10 metres in diameter, through which water flows at 1,200 litres per second from the Aniene into a huge pond situated above the Ovato fountain. For the supply of the palace and the upper garden, he channelled water from the Rivellese spring into large tanks in the palace courtyard. He had calculated in every last detail the volume and natural pressure of the water required to supply the fifty fountains of the villa.

For a better understanding of the Neapolitan architect's outstanding achievement, it should be recalled that, also in those times, all the water effects (jets, sprays, fans, etc.) were obtained by exploitation only of the communicating-basin principles, without any resort whatsoever to motive power. Ligorio enjoyed the collaboration also of hydraulic experts of the calibre of Giacomo della Porta and the Frenchman Claude Venard who designed the prodigious water system of the Organ fountain.

With the completion of the technical work, the ornamental fountains were built and the scene enhanced by the placing

The Pegasus Fountain ▶
This circular fountain is situated to the right of the foot of the stairway from the villa. The mythological winged horse seems to be taking flight from the supporting rock.

The Organ Fountain ▶
Designed by Pirrin del Gagliardo, this fountain contains the amazing hydraulic organ (no longer functioning) created by the Frenchman Venard. From a large toothed-cylinder water was projected on to the keys of an organ manual, thus sounding the carillon. The incredulous Gregory XIII had to make sure that no one was hidden within the device to produce the music.

The Fishponds

Turning from the Organ fountain, there below, among the foliage, is the series of large fishponds. Although less picturesque than the scene from below, this view-point provides a fine panorama of the water effects created by the imaginative designer of Villa d'Este.

The Cypress Rotunda

At the centre of the lower park is a stupendous rotunda, surrounded by enormous centuries-old cypresses, replacing the arbours and wooden kiosk which once greeted guests upon entering the villa. From here they could glimpse the splendour of the palace above, through tree-tops and the majestic play of water.

▼   ▶

at carefully selected points of Roman statues excavated in the nearby Hadrian's Villa.

The visitor cannot fail to be entranced by the continuous alternation of water and greenery, with a fresh surprise around every corner, by the harmony of the wondrously varied setting of this theatre which is Villa d'Este. But perhaps, in his bewilderment, he loses sight of the real measure of its magnificence; and no catalogue, enumerating the hydraulic installations, the flora, can do justice to the technical miracle created by Pirro Ligorio and his colleagues, involving a multitude of intricate solutions. But the living testimony to their unrivalled achievement of four hundred years ago is there, in the shade of centuries-old cypresses.

◄◄

The Fountain of Nature
Gillo della Vellita's fine statue of Diana of Ephesus, symbol of fertility, once adorned the Organ fountain: from the lower park, facing Rome, it now reigns supreme.

◄

The Mete Fountain
This large formless fountain, with water trickling over its moss-covered rocks, symbolizes the Meta Sudante, once situated alongside Constantine's Arch in Rome, where the gladiators used to wash after combat in the circus.

◄

The Ariadne Fountain
Situated on a terrace offering a panorama of the Tivoli countryside, this fountain unfortunately no longer contains the statue of the sleeping Ariadne which once adorned the central recess.

250	sprays
50	jets
55	fans
290	nozzles
60	springs
250	waterfalls
100	ponds
100	ramps, totalling 350 metres in length
50	fountains
20	stairways, totalling 500 steps
20	terraces and exedras
500	gate valves of varying size
300	sluice valves
200	water filters
20,000	flower vases, fixed or movable
30,000	seasonally-rotating plants
150	centuries-old tall trees
15,000	perennial ornamental trees and shrubs
4,000	metres of espaliers and box-hedges
9,000	square metres of avenues, paths and slopes
35,000	square metres, total area of garden
1,200	litres of water per second drawn from River Aniene

Medieval Tivoli

From the terraces running along the perimeter of the park, enhanced by small fountains, is a panorama of the roads leading down from Tivoli to the plain, with many well-preserved Medieval houses. Pirro Ligorio had part of this district, Valle Gaudente, demolished to provide space for the park.

▼

The Fishponds

The three large ponds, with 48 water-jets, were once used for breeding trout and other delectable fish for banquets given for the Cardinals' guests. In the background is Neptune's fountain and, above, the Organ fountain.

▶

The Este Eagles

This fountain, to the left of the fishponds, is clearly inspired by the eagles which, together with the fleur-de-lis, constituted the coat-of-arms of the House of Este. The two themes appear frequently in the sculptures and decorations of the villa.

The Neptune Fountain

This majestic water display is the sole modern contribution to the garden. The fountain was built in 1927, incorporating an incomplete torso of the God Neptune, which was intended for the exedra adjoining the terrace, but was placed in the recess veiled by the central cascade of water.

▼   ▼▶

The artistic creator of Villa d'Este

It is of course impossible to list all the painters, sculptors, potters, mosaicists, engineers, architects, decorators, master craftsmen who, over the years, created Villa d'Este. The central protagonist was, as we have seen, Pirro Ligorio: but as regards the hydraulic works, mention must be made of Tommaso da Siena, creator of fanciful water effects, the Frenchman Claude Venard, inventor of the water organ, and Giovanni del Luca, responsible for the Owl fountain.

Outstanding among the fountain designers are Pirrin del Gagliardo (Organ fountain), Orazio Olivieri (Dragon fountain) and Raffaele Sangallo (who completed the Owl fountain). The statues of Diana of Ephesus and the Albunea Sibyl are by Gillo della Vellita, the Grotto of Diana by Curzio Maccarone and Lola and Paolo Calandrino, while the statues of the Rivers Aniene and Ercolano are probably by Giovanni Malanca. Some also attribute to Bernini the Wineglass fountain.

As to the internal decor of the palace, highly important roles were played by Taddeo and Federico Zuccari (Mannerists from Pesaro), Livio Agresti (of Forlì) and Girolamo Muziano (of Brescia), founder in 1577 of the S. Luca Academy. They were largely responsible for the decoration of the various rooms, which also contain frescoes by Tempesta, by the Belgian Karcher, and a portrait of Cardinal Farnese, attributed to Perin del Vaga. The magnificent wooden ceiling of the Cardinals' Room is the work of the Flemish Flaminio Bolinger. Little remains of the statues and precious works, by artists such as Benvenuto Cellini, which once adorned the palace. And then there were the many famous scholars, poets, artists and, particularly, musicians who enjoyed the patronage and hospitality of the House of Este: they were received in the Agevoli Academy, founded in Tivoli in 1571. Ippolito II was without doubt a devotee of music: he protected and helped the « maestro of stringed instruments » Nicola Vicentino, the talented Pierluigi da Palestrina, Francesco Portinaro, Soto, Golia, Buonaugurio. There was never a conference or reception at Villa d'Este that was not enlivened by concerts or the singing of madrigals: music was not a corollary, but an essential component of a pleasurable sublimation of human gifts in the search of beauty.

▶

The Girandola Fountain
This wider perspective provides a fuller concept of the Renaissance style of the « Catherine-wheel », (or Dragon) fountain illustrated on page 15.

▶

The « Cordonata dei Bollori »
Rising gently from the right of the Girandola fountain is this enchanting flight of steps, at its sides water bubbling from a series of small basins, creating the impression of boiling water. Hence the strange name of this fascinating creation, literally, « The Boiling-water Steps ».

The Owl Fountain

The pleasant avenue, famed for its hydrangeas, between the Dragon fountain and the « Cordonata » leads to this unusual fountain by G. del Luca. A remarkable water-driven device caused a bronze owl to appear at intervals, emitting a shriek which silenced the twittering, created by water under pressure, of bronze birds resting on branches. Unfortunately, the device is now lost.

The Persephone Fountain

This fountain is situated to the left of the Owl fountain. Its centrepiece, in a recess, is a horse-drawn shell-shaped boat, which is carrying Persephone, abducted by Pluto, to the Lower Regions.

The two flanking flights of steps lead up to a large terrace, the site of the « Rometta » (literally, « Rome in miniature ») spectacle.

The Rometta Waterfall

Above, between rocks and foliage, a statue of the River Aniene, supporting the Sibyl Temple, marks the beginning of a waterfall which cascades through a fascinating miniaturized reproduction of celebrated Roman monuments and allegories. The scene once served as the « backcloth » of a small theatre.

▼ ▼ ▶

The Rometta spectacle.

The Statue of the Goddess Rome.

The Rometta

The allegorical course of the Aniene into the Tiber, and of the latter through Rome, is strewn with small-scale ancient monuments (Pantheon, Augustus Mausoleum, Colosseum). Lower down, where the water course widens, is Isola Tiberina, in the form of a ship. Above is Pierre La Motte's statue of the Goddess Rome, with the she-wolf suckling Romulus and Remus.

The Hundred Fountains

This third major avenue crossing the garden leads from the Rometta complex to the magnificent Ovato fountain. One hundred metres long, it is flanked on the right by two superimposed series of basins, into which water bubbles from a myriad of jets. Pirro Ligorio, who personally designed the avenue, crowned the effect with ships, obelisks,

◀   ▼

and the fleur-de-lis emblem of the House of Este. From above, water leaping from a series of small fountains further enhances the incomparable scene. Ligorio's masterpiece was embellished in 1685 by Francesco II of Modena, with the addition of the stone eagles, completing the Este coat-of-arms.

Originally the fountains were decorated with stuccoes, but over the years they have almost all disappeared.

To the left of the avenue strange sphinxes and marine monsters complete the breathtaking spectacle, which inspired even Gabriele d'Annunzio to write some moving verses. The original scenic fascination is nowadays enhanced at night by an imaginative lighting scheme, leaving the visitor with an unforgettable memory of the avenue.

At its end, in full majesty, is the Queen of the Villa d'Este fountains, the Ovato.

The Ovato, Queen of Fountains

The Ovato fountain (so called from its oval shape) is without doubt Pirro Ligorio's finest creation, with its exquisite blend of natural beauty and architectural skill. Drawn from the Aniene, the water flows into the pool and then supplies almost the entire garden. Above, between two Tartarean rocks, is G. della Vellita's Sibyl and the Aniene and Ercolano statues. A marble Genie floats in the centre of the pool. The ten arches of the exedra running around the rear of the pool contain naiads by G. B. della Porta. From behind the iridescent screen of the semicircular waterfall is yet another fascinating view of the Avenue of the Hundred Fountains. The external face of the wall around the pool is decorated with majolica tiles bearing the eagles and fleur-de-lis of the Este family.

The Aniene and the Sibyl.

The Ovato fountain from above, by night.

The Wineglass Fountain

The third major feature of the central avenue leading up to the villa, after the Cypress Rotunda and the Dragon fountain, this 17th century style work consists of a large conch-shaped base supporting a floral stone chalice emitting frothing water. Style-wise, many experts attribute the fountain to G. Lorenzo Bernini, but there is no final certainty as to its creator.

The Diana Grotto

Situated at the far right of the supporting wall of the Palla-corda terrace, this magnificent work is richly decorated with stuccoes, mosaics and reliefs portraying scenes from mythology by Curzio Maccarone and Lola and Paolo Calandrino. There are also portrayals of Minerva, Neptune, the Muses and caryatids bearing baskets of fruit.

The Central Hall of the Nobile Apartment.

The villa

The illustrious guests of Ippolito II entered Villa d'Este from the lower garden, on the road from Rome: and for sure, they must have been entranced as they made their way up to the villa through the park, exquisitely designed by Ligorio. Having ascended the double staircase at the top of the park they entered the central hall of the Nobile Apartment, its ceiling heightened by the perspective of the supporting columns. Then they would proceed to the Throne Room, from the splendid balcony of which they were presented with a breathtaking view, rich in colour from the vivid green of the park, interspersed with statuary from Imperial homes, while in the distance lay Rome, bathed in sun: a truly enchanting and unforgettable scene. Today, unfortunately, the villa no longer has its tapestries, plush sofas, furniture, candlesticks and other trappings: but the fine frescoes and imposing architecture recall much of its former splendour.

The central hall, its magnificent ceiling with Muziano's Banquet of the Gods (completed by F. Zuccari), contains a fountain with caryatids, the original plan of Villa d'Este, two amusing simulated doors with paintings of a Renaissance nobleman and a woman with leopard.

The first of the suite of four rooms on the right contains the Labours of Hercules (Muziano and Karcher); then comes the Hall of the Philosophers and Hall of the Glory of Este (F. Zuccari) and the Hunting Room, with scenes frescoed by Tempesta. The first two rooms of the suite on the left are decorated by Agresti, inspired by the mythical origins of Tivoli; the last two contain Muziano's works depicting biblical stories of Noah and Moses.

On the second floor is the Old Apartment, its centrepiece the Throne Room and balcony. The second room on the left, with Bolinger's splendid wooden ceiling, was once the Cardinals' bedroom, adjoining a richly-stuccoed chapel. With the antique furniture and paintings arranged beneath Agresti's ceilings, this floor is nowadays a small art gallery.

The last fountain (with reclining Venus) is found in the Benedictine cloister of the original convent, the source of the ambitious dream of the Este family. The cloister leads into

▶

The Nobile Apartment
The caryatid fountain in the central hall. Within the recess is a mosaic of the Temple of the Sibyl, the symbol of Tivoli.

▶▶

The Council of the Gods
This fresco is the central panel of the ceiling in the room of the « Labours of Hercules », by Muziano and Karcher.

▶

The Philosophers' Hall
The allegorical frescoes of virtue, nature, the arts and sciences are attributed to Federico Zuccari and his school.

Hall of the Glory of Este

Inspired by the splendour of the family of Cardinals, the decoration of this room (the third of the right-hand suite of the Nobile Apartment) is also attributed to Federico Zuccari and his school.

The Throne Room

This central room of the old apartment, on the upper floor of the villa, leads on to a balcony with a magnificent view. The four ceiling panels contain views of the Aniene and of Tivoli. On the walls: Raffaele's copy of a portrait of Julius II, the Holy Family, and Card. Farnese by Perin del Vaga, a Madonna attributed to A. del Sarto.

Nobile Apartment: Room of Tiburtine Mythology, by L. Agresti.

Tiburto sacrifices to the Gods (L. Agresti).

Ceiling of Cardinals' bedroom (Flaminio Bolinger).

◀

Tiburtine Mythology
by Livio Agresti
The Etruscan King Anio, pursuing Cetego, drowns in the River Parensio: the present name of the river derives from this episode.

The Cloister of the Villa ▼ ▼
The old Benedictine cloister, restored by Raffaello da Firenze, contains the fountain of Venus, portraying the sleeping Goddess.

The Aniene waterfall in Villa Gregoriana.

Villa Gregoriana

The River Aniene has always played a notable role in the history of Tivoli: but although on the whole it has been a favourable role — because the artistic life and fortunes of the town are founded on its river — this lively water course has certainly not spared the Tiburtines of grief and disaster.

Way back in ancient times the river, hurtling down towards Rome between the lower slopes of Monte Catillo and the dwellings of the citadel, was continuously eroding the sub-soil of the Acropolis, threatening even the Temple of Vesta and the Temple of the Sibyl. In 105 A. D. a catastrophic flood caused the collapse of part of the hillside over the waterfall, sweeping away many Roman dwellings, including the splendid villa of the poet Manlio Vopisco. During the subsequent centuries the river's fury was somewhat tamed, but it continued to eat away the rocks and never ceased to be a serious threat to the town.

And then, on November 16, 1826, in full flood, the Aniene demolished the dam to the side of the town: the underlying waterfalls disappeared and the river carried away most of the left bank and many of the buildings of the Santa Lucia quarter.

The government of Leon II repaired the damage as far as possible, but a definitive solution was not found until 1832, when Clemente Folchi presented Pope Gregory XVI with a revolutionary project: to divert the course of the Aniene by tunnelling through Monte Catillo higher above the town, moving the head of water so as to form an artificial lake. On October 7, 1835 the Pope witnessed the awe-striking spectacle

Villa Gregoriana

Back in 1809 General Miollis, Napoleonic Governor of Rome, had a path cut in the rocks to enable descent to the gorge of the Aniene. Gregory XVI continued the project, rendering access to the natural park containing the remains of bridges, buildings and sepulchral pillars of Roman times. Along its narrow avenues one reaches two splendid but awesome grottoes, one known as Neptune the other as the Sirens, through which flows the water of the Bernini tributary down to the Aniene.

as the river, diverted through the new 300 metre long tunnels, thundered for the first time down the new 120 metre high waterfalls. All around the waterfalls major restoration work was carried out on the present Villa Gregoriana: a park of rare natural beauty was created, offering an impressive view of the temples, still standing on the Acropolis, and, beneath, of the huge waterfalls immersed in woodland, thereby accentuating the centuries-old violence of the cascading water.

From the hydroelectric station at the foot of the waterfalls, on July 4, 1892, *for the first time in the world,* electric power was transmitted over a distance: from the massive head of the Aniene to illuminate Rome.

The Aniene Waterfall
The water of the Aniene hurtles over the 120 metres high waterfall, in a setting of completely unspoilt natural beauty.

Hadrian's Villa: Canopus, Statue of Mars.

Hadrian's Imperial Villa

« If the Greeks found the temple, the dwelling of the Gods, inhospitable to man, in Rome the dwellings of men had to be fit, if necessary, to entertain the Gods ». The meaning of this discerning observation made by G. B. Salerno is at once evident to all who approach the majestic remains of what was one of the most advanced expressions of Roman art and without doubt the grandest of the luxurious Imperial homes.

Built between 121 and 137 A. D., as the impressions on the bricks still testify, Hadrian's palace represents the realization of the dreams and ambitions of this eclectic Emperor-architect, who bequeathed to the world the 117 km of « Vallum Hadriani » in Britain and his magnificent Mausoleum, today the mighty foundations of Castel S. Angelo.

Born in 76 A. D. near Seville, adopted by Trajan, whom he succeeded in 117, Hadrian's overriding sense of the rule of law created in him the desire to unify, politically and administratively, an empire of one hundred million subjects. He started to travel widely, to understand, to pacify, to amalgamate: and from every journey, especially in the Greek world, he gained new invigorating impresssions of life and the arts, which fundamentally influenced everything he achieved in the indulgence of his overwhelming passion, architecture.

And so Hadrian transformed this area of three hundred hectares into a splendid palace and gardens, incorporating styles from all the places he had seen on his travels, blending the pure movement of the boldly liberal Hellenistic art with the advanced techniques characteristic of Roman architecture. With the exploitation of the vault and the arch, spatial architecture

The Pecile ▶
The pool was the centrepiece of a square colonnade, of which only the northern outer wall (9 metres high) remains. Still visible at its top are the recesses which bore the beams of the 97 x 232 m colonnade.

The Baths ▶
Bold arched vaults once formed the ceiling of an apse-shaped hall with swimming pool, columns, stuccoes and fine mosaic floors.

had arrived: with Hadrian, space became a function of the environment, the expression of the highest spiritual values.

In other words, basing his concepts on the « divine proportions » of Vitruvio and Rabirio, he was seeking an art form that was at once universal and enlightened. This remains the underlying significance of the Imperial palace, even if the decorative superstructure was not at the same exquisite level.

Statues, stuccoes, mosaics and frescoes do not sufficiently reflect the evolutionary zeal of the Emperor: but although they may be typical manifestations of decadent Hellenistic art, for centuries they were the prey of plunderers of every kind. During the Dark Ages, the Tiburtines used the villa as a source of building materials: hundreds of valuable items were carried off to museums throughout the world or to other stately homes; but much of importance remains, and excavations are continuing to bring to light the many treasures that certainly lie hidden beneath the olive groves on the lower slopes of Tivoli.

The lay-out of Hadrian's Villa much resembled that of an authentic township: there were services such as a fire station,

▲

Architect Italo Gismondi's model provides an overall idea of the splendour of the villa.

▶

The Canopus

Inspired by the canal between Alexandria and Canopus in the Nile Delta, the complex once contained a copy of the temple of the Goddess Serapis. A colonnade with statues surrounded the 18 x 119 m pool. On one side are six caryatids (as in the Erechtheum of Athens) and two Silenus.

Maritime Theatre
Three views of the 134 m circumference colonnade with 40 Ionic columns. Hadrian used to retire to study in the small central island with courtyard and gardens.

The Pecile Wall
The massive northern wall of the pool, seen by night.

Remains of the Hall of Doric Columns.

Avenue near the wall of the Double Colonnade.

the barracks of the Imperial guard, housing for the villa staff and servants, kitchens, storehouses, cattlesheds.

There were gardens, swimming pools, fountains without end, and here, too, the water of the Aniene was indispensable: then there were two large bath complexes, complete with sun-bathing lounges, sauna baths, colonnaded frigidarium, central heating, and perfect water-supply, drainage and sewage systems. For the energetically-inclined there was a stadium, race-course and gymnasium: then there were two theatres, two libraries, a college, as well as basilicas and temples for spiritual elevation and contemplative solitude.

There were rationally designed buildings, such as the warehouses and staff living quarters, the guest house. And naturally, the most grandiose of all was the Imperial residence, with its huge reception halls, such as the vestibule facing the Golden Square, together with superb terraces and colonnades overlooking enchanting landscapes.

On all sides were statues of Gods and heroes, sphinxes and idols, in fine multicoloured marble: and although most of the splendid mosaic floors have been plundered, there still remains, in total, almost half an hectare! Then there were examples of the styles Hadrian borrowed from around the world: the Lyceum, the Prytaneum, the Academy; the Pecile, a huge square colonnade inspired by the Stoa Poikile in Athens; the Canopus, a fine pool surrounded by columns and statues, inspired by the city on the Nile, destination of pilgrim worshippers of the faith-healing Goddess Serapis; the Odeum, and even Hades.

Environments and settings in which the memory of the original was merely a pretext to set free the imagination of the Emperor aesthete in his unceasing quest for innovative planimetries, graceful curves of walls and colonnades, the bold sweep of vaults and arches, for new art forms in the context of a continuing play of balanced spaces, blended with observance of a sound Classicist ideal.

A world of dreams which we, too, can experience as we wander through the majestic ruins, midst the rustling of the centuries-old cypresses of the Greek Theatre, the while swans glide silently in the shadows cast by the caryatids of the Canopus.

The dreams of Caesar Trajan Hadrian Augustus, the builder who « used as his binding element a blend of human virtues, science and beauty ».

The Pecile Wall: 6,000 sq. m. of « opus reticulatum ».

Bibliography:

Renzo Mosti
History and Monuments of Tivoli
Soc. Tib. St. Arte, 1968

Vincenzo Pacifici
Medieval Tivoli
Atti e Mem. Tiburtini, voll. V-VI, 1925-1926

Carlo Regnoni Macera
Banners of the Quarters of Tivoli
Atti e mem. Tiburtini, voll. XXII-XXIII, 1959-1960

Official guide
Villa d'Este at Tivoli
Oto, Roma, 1971

Giuseppe Radiciotti
Music in Villa d'Este
Atti e Mem. Tiburtini

Villa Gregoriana
Atti e Mem. Tiburtini, vol. XV, 1939

Camillo Pierattini
The Emperor Hadrian at Tivoli
Atti e Mem. Tiburtini, vol. XXXVII, 1964

Giovan Battista Salerno
Appreciation of Hadrian's Villa
Atti e Mem. Tiburtini, vol. XXVII, 1954

The publishers wish to express their gratitude to the Lazio Historic Monuments Authority and the Società Tiburtina di Storia e d'Arte for their valuable cooperation in the production of this publication.

Organizational assistant: Santino Bricca